**CURATOR
OF EPHEMERA
AT THE
NEW MUSEUM FOR
ARCHAIC MEDIA**

American Indian Studies Series

Gordon Henry, SERIES EDITOR

Bawaajimo: *A Dialect of Dreams in Anishinaabe Language and Literature*,
Margaret Noodin | 978-1-61186-105-1

Centering Anishinaabeg Studies: Understanding the World through Stories, edited by
Jill Doerfler, Niigaanwewidam James Sinclair, and Heidi Kiiwetinepinesiik Stark |
978-1-61186-067-2

Curator of Ephemera at the New Museum for Archaic Media, Heid E. Erdrich |
978-1-61186-246-1

Document of Expectations, Devon Abbott Mihesuah | 978-1-61186-011-5

Dragonfly Dance, Denise K. Lajimodiere | 978-0-87013-982-6

Facing the Future: The Indian Child Welfare Act at 30, edited by Matthew L. M. Fletcher,
Wenona T. Singel, and Kathryn E. Fort | 978-0-87013-860-7

Follow the Blackbirds, Gwen Nell Westerman | 978-1-61186-092-4

Indian Country: Telling a Story in a Digital Age, Victoria L. LaPoe and
Benjamin Rex LaPoe II | 978-1-61186-226-3

The Indian Who Bombed Berlin and Other Stories, Ralph Salisbury | 978-0-87013-847-8

Masculindians: Conversations about Indigenous Manhood, edited by Sam McKegney |
978-1-61186-129-7

Mediating Indianness, edited by Cathy Covell Waegner | 978-1-61186-151-8

The Murder of Joe White: Ojibwe Leadership and Colonialism in Wisconsin, Erik M. Redix |
978-1-61186-145-7

National Monuments, Heid E. Erdrich | 978-0-87013-848-5

Ogimawkwe Mitigwaki (*Queen of the Woods*), Simon Pokagon | 978-0-87013-987-1

Ottawa Stories from the Springs: anishinaabe dibaadjimowinan wodi gaa binjibaamigak wodi mookodjiwong e zhinikaadek, translated and edited by Howard Webkamigad | 978-1-61186-137-2

Plain of Jars and Other Stories, Geary Hobson | 978-0-87013-998-7

Sacred Wilderness, Susan Power | 978-1-61186-111-2

Seeing Red—Hollywood's Pixeled Skins: American Indians and Film, edited by LeAnne Howe, Harvey Markowitz, and Denise K. Cummings | 978-1-61186-081-8

Shedding Skins: Four Sioux Poets, edited by Adrian C. Louis | 978-0-87013-823-2

Sounding Thunder: The Stories of Francis Pegahmagabow, Brian D. McInnes | 978-1-61186-225-6

Stories for a Lost Child, Carter Meland | 978-1-61186-244-7

Stories through Theories/Theories through Stories: North American Indian Writing, Storytelling, and Critique, edited by Gordon D. Henry Jr., Nieves Pascual Soler, and Silvia Martinez-Falquina | 978-0-87013-841-6

That Guy Wolf Dancing, Elizabeth Cook-Lynn | 978-1-61186-138-9

Those Who Belong: Identity, Family, Blood, and Citizenship among the White Earth Anishinaabeg, Jill Doerfler | 978-1-61186-169-3

Visualities: Perspectives on Contemporary American Indian Film and Art, edited by Denise K. Cummings | 978-0-87013-999-4

Writing Home: Indigenous Narratives of Resistance, Michael D. Wilson | 978-0-87013-818-8

Michigan State University Press   *East Lansing*

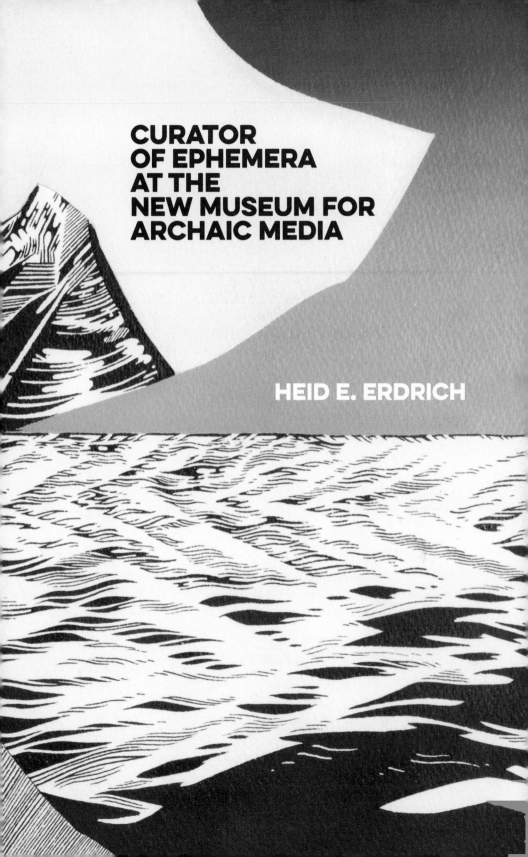

CURATOR
OF EPHEMERA
AT THE
NEW MUSEUM FOR
ARCHAIC MEDIA

HEID E. ERDRICH

♾ The paper used in this publication meets the minimum
requirements of ANSI/NISO Z39.48-1992 (R 1997) (Permanence
of Paper).

Michigan State University Press
East Lansing, Michigan 48823-5245

Printed and bound in the United States of America.

26 25 24 23 22 21 20 19 18 17   1 2 3 4 5 6 7 8 9 10

Library of Congress Cataloging-in-Publication Data
Names: Erdrich, Heid E. (Heid Ellen) author.
Title: Curator of ephemera at the New Museum for Archaic Media /
    Heid E. Erdrich.
Description: East Lansing : Michigan State University Press, [2017] |
    Series: American Indian studies series
Identifiers: LCCN 2016036973| ISBN 9781611862461 (pbk. : alk. paper) |
    ISBN 9781609175283 (pdf) | ISBN 9781628952988 (epub) |
    ISBN 9781628962987 (kindle)
Classification: LCC PS3555.R418 A6 2017 | DDC 811/.54   dc23
LC record available at https://lccn.loc.gov/2016036973

Cover and book design by Erin Kirk New.
Cover artwork is a detail from *Ink Babel* (2015) by Andrea Carlson and
is used with permission. All rights reserved.

g green press INITIATIVE Michigan State University Press is a member of
the Green Press Initiative and is committed to
developing and encouraging ecologically responsible publishing
practices. For more information about the Green Press Initiative
and the use of recycled paper in book publishing, please visit www.
greenpressinitiative.org.

Visit Michigan State University Press at www.msupress.org

This book is made animate

with gratitude for the artwork

and lifework of Jonathan Thunder.

Thank you, my co-creator,

brother, and friend.

To the collaborative spirit

of my sister Anishinaabekweg—

Andrea Carlson, Elizabeth Day,

and Margaret Noodin

Contents

QR codes are included in this book
to allow access to another form of
the poems contained here. QR code
reader apps are readily available as
free downloads. You can also view all
of Heid E. Erdrich's poemeos on her
Vimeo and YouTube channels.

PERMANENT
INSTALLATION

Curatorial Statement for *Wiindigo Eye*

Viewing this work through the lens of Fresnel, an oblique critical angle might be arrived at, and we may appreciate the layers of flat and curved surface, the distinct cultural experience refracted in black and white. Each section of the whole builds imaging and non-imaging so that areas of text, "there's a picture opposite me / of my primitive ancestry / that stood on rocky shores and kept the beaches shipwreck free," might act as non-image. Convexly, the artist's DNA— left as she crimped the paper, sucked the brush to a fine tip, hiccupped, tore a nail—creates an image of the indigenous corpus. That this image arises entirely from non-visible elements, and yet we see figures we relate to our engagement, surely shows the work itself commands us to interact with it. That the type of interaction is not specified means less than that we viewers scrape the underside of well-muscled 100 pound paper, send the sample, and await results. Or as critic Jessica Kolopenuk asserts: . . . *they can learn their "true ancestry"—they can now feast on the genetic contents of their own flesh. They have themselves become host to the* wiindigo.

The Honey Suckers

We drank the nectar left there for you
We grew drunk on doom

There was never enough

Down by the river of our youth
we pulled love with our tongues

We took something from you

Green-groping in reeds and stink
river slow in its drive-by saw us

said nothing   We could say
we were young—young was once true

We took all that was sweet and all that would be
We left no excuse

We ignored the body-made call   .   the sweet text
its subtle, alien speech

We beseeched! We beseeched!
Did you not get our message?
It tasted of many grasses drunk
clover bud, sepal, petals—
then panic, then wrath, then the end

All that we read
we misread

Come hither, help us! Come-come!
Did you not get enough?
Taste in the grass, be drunk—
Taste many times over   taste more
taste in hurry   in passion
taste to the end of all tongues and be done

Autobiography as Gesture

All that I meant   All my intent   What I had to say

carpal tunnel pulses a flow of sparks so I print with light on light   indelible
information encodes then deletes   still the paths in my hands
faint remains   no   not as if sparks in the dark liquid of mind could
express   impress this last medium—

delete to the bone   bone's deep chambers   down to what's left   what's been left
our bodies   nothing less

our hands   the thumb beloved   gesture trace—other's touch   destroying breath

fluted traces in ancestral caves   women and children on rainy days   finger waves
in clay   a mania of hands   akimbo   askance   verbal as dance
they touched and touched and touched

do not touch

What I had to say I   intend not portend

        in sign and shrug   implied   vibe   eye-stray   key cached   digital capture
        smoke and signal   blown through hand-formed bone hoop
        bite and bark   birch cutouts of my dream-song   template for black bear
        humpback and hunch of wolverine—

My head tilts   my eye bats   my breath lets   frets across millennia   delicate
antiquities   try not to breathe   future fragility   not to touch

All that I meant   All my intent   What I had to say I
stroked instead.

Wireless Handshake

Drums talking   they say   or smoke signals   we used long ago
like Pope Smoke   dark or white

or the prairies fired to say we've entered near   we are here we are here we are here
Whale Smoke when we needed crowds   to take the meat before the tide

or the Noon Gun signaling military time
                ancestor of the factory whistle   school bell

What we wanted to know   I asked

Now give me your reply   pick your mode   sync   syn

Photophone   Radiophone Videophone   Satellite stuttering high
Shortwave   Microwave
Heliograph   of sun and mirrors or moon and mirrors

Lighthouse   Beacon fire   Balefire
a pillar of cloud by day . . . a pillar of fire by night
Landing lights   Aldis lamp   shuttering flashes of code

What we wanted to know   I ack   I ask   I syn ack   you know

Now give me your reply   pick your mode
Cellular   Mobile Device
Or come quite close
        stroke my hair aside
                buzz the cilia deep in my ear

my neck   your Vampire Tap   Lightning   Thunderbolt

Unless   too wired   too tied to copper   you choose to co-
axially   to Cat 5   Your choice
Unshielded Twisted Pair   or   Shielded Twisted Pair

We be either or both   just text me which   so we sync
     what we wanted to sync
               so flood follows   serves   us   for you
                                                            not one thing would I deny

Undead Faerie Goes Great with India Pale Ale

Pale and smoky eye
                puny bruised bully
thin as a wing—
                victim rampant
                in a fierce corset

That look, I've never liked

Shards of black lace or
tattered chiffon trailing
over an arm brace
                and a crossbow

Lidded glances, that look I know
That look comes around
                every decade or so

Panting waxy vampires, sexy undead

Hipster Zombies
Ravishing Aliens
Punk Voodoo Queens

Goth go-eth before
                and after
                the fall

And we've seen it all before
Only this time the tenor shifts—

What we know: we are already eating each other
We are already part of this

Plaid-skirted co-eds at colleges in the seventies
                              we ate them
Drunken Midwestern youths by the quarry   we devoured
                                        by the score

We are already eating each other
We are already part of this

Mother's veins open, bleed copper and black
                              leave a sheen on our lips
We lick, then start in again
Machines drink and drink what we think is clean

Already eating each other we are already
part of this

Mouth-feel is all, gorgeous umami,
tender children, veal in a school bus
                              we are eating you all right now

I myself have eaten you all already
                        with fries and a beer

You did not satisfy

What I want now is an Undead Faerie—
                        a palate cleanser
a poof of foam   squid ink in whisked cream
pomegranate syrup in salty swirls
                        that bleed deeply
tasty yes, but an hour later . . .

We are already eating each other
We are already a part of this

Red Star

Inside the red star of a cottonwood twig
inside the box of the North Dakota map
that is my country

my country as it was

Two-hundred-year-old towers
trees old as our sorrow
their silver leaves platter
for no one now

Two-hundred-year-old trees
lost their way to breed

their old gray branches
no longer strong enough
to hold our dead

Sweet embrace of eternal sleep
lovers' arms always   always   always
now no more

No longer strong enough
to hold our ancestors
in their sleep
silver leaves platter for no one now

Inside the red star of a cottonwood heart
inside the box of the North Dakota map—

Sixty years the dams
kept these trees
raining clouds of seed
on barren silt

There will be no more great cottonwoods

There is nowhere left to go to die
but the boxy map of my country
in the red star of my deep inside

Inside cottonwood twigs is the shape of a star. A sign of life and
natural harmony for American Indians and others, cottonwood
forests along the Missouri River are in decline.
—Brian Gehring, *Bismarck Tribune,* October 13, 2013

The Gig of Light

Let us now speak of The Gig of Light

Let us speak as the buzz of bulbs   brilliantly or
vividly intoned as old-timers' concert flashbacks

Let our memoir-a-thon glitter and flit
Firefly-in-the-face vs. flash-in-the-pan

Let us speak long of The Gig of Light

How we held the retina in a dazzle—
how we zapped the sun up for a second
how we shocked with watts
and perfect resolution

Oh, The Gig of Light! The Gig of Light!

How we shimmered
aurora-like and arousing
how we glowed
green-blue and crisp
how we flickered
meaningfully or with menace—

How we streaked across the screen
and were seen no more

Boom

Pale wool   blue horizon design   an itchy landscape
We all wore the same bargain sweater
in an airplane   in a dream   Boom   A fight erupts

Take your seats please, and can we have peace?
No more argument from you Mister
Mr. Not-Our-Same-Sweater-Wearer

The radio wakes me with its cultured accent
"The Labor Department today said . . ."
Push   *Push*   *Push*   my beloved urges
as he snaps it to snooze

Snow and silence fill things
with nothing

Still, stillness is something

Swirls of subconscious speak still
so early my yearning bares itself
prairie   butte   air so huge you gulp

you might go down   drown from so much sky
Such perfect absence   There's nothing there but
birds whirling   snow geese as far as the eye sees

North Dakota winds in grassland
now that's constancy   Buffalo grass glows
frosted   flowing   speaking low   secretive

Used to be there was nothing there
Close it up   they used to say
Return it to the Buffalo   Forget Indians

Wind churns a million watts
Gas burns ancient marshes off
Coal pits deep and busy   like messy little cities

Tell you what, drive out at night
This is what an engineer in Fargo urges
Flares for miles   he promises   *as far as the eye . . .*

Boom

The Dark Sky Reserve

Say what you will   silent lake

wimpy shimmer of clouds
shrugging a blueness   a blank slate

non-verbal pre-verbal verb-less breathless expectation

Jet trails uncross the air
so sky no more hatches
plans to own itself

                   it owns itself

                   reservation by mistake
reserved for our escape
because it is sky   because it is space

Hang Fire

Depth of dark air between us
we sense all things suspended

How tenderly we glance at Earth in her black velvet

Little strings of farmyard lights outside tiny prairie towns
—glitter of lit roads appear to adorn her

How tender our sentiment at cruising altitude—
as soon as we've taken off, we want her back

Depth of heaven beneath us
we sense nothing and all between

We wonder what's out there—

Then intercede the flares
a hundred miles of red eyes
a forever of red lights that thin but do not end

where once the darkest dark dropped through to still more dark
where even a new moon could reflect in our eyes
where that gleam alone could be our guide
out of sage scent and tumbled canyon   out of a constant quiet

Out of that profound suspension
relieved of all things human

reason became quickening became our fire

Our own fire

—lit in a pact we made with the sky

Soon our gaze strayed from the sky to flickers of ideas sparks of stories
embers of memory we banked to make a future   to fashion foolish notions

How quickly we returned to gazing as if above it
                    turned all to sentiment   all suspended

Once we own it
                    we cannot un-own our fire

Once we suspended fire in the night sky
                    we could no longer see in the dark and darkness deserted us
                    we knew then the infinity of our fire and how our fire hangs on us

How we must hang with fire

Our burning night sky shames us to the world. It is prairie skies
that define a prairie landscape, as well as a prairie inhabitant.
Desecration of those skies runs contrary to our conservative
character and native quickening.
—Jan Swenson, Badlands Conservation Alliance,
    quoted in *Native Sun News*, February 2015

These Are My Pearls, This Is My Swine

Pale soap bubble accreted around grit
Irritation gone iridescent   gone global

These are my pearls   this is my swine

Unleash the tuxedo pigs   attired so fine
Let boars fork these pearls like truffles
tusked from prairie sand

These are my pearls   this is my swine
These my words   my copper mine

Like the base who threw away
the worth of all his tribe
wealth we sign away line by line

These are my pearls   this is my swine

Dress me in the blood shawl   drape the shells
in a graduated rope around my neck
Tell them it is time   Open the door
invite the oil-rich and velvet-dressed swine

These are my pearls   I have made them mine

Pre-Occupied

River   river   river
I never   never   never
etched your spiral icon in limestone
or   for that matter   pitched a tent on cement
near your banks

Banks of marble   stock still   all movement in the plaza
river walking its message on an avenue
rallied in bitter wind

Excuse my digression   my mind tends ...

In reality   my screen is lit with invitations
bake a casserole—send pizza—make soup for the 99%

Sorry   somehow I haven't time

Flow   flow   flow both ways in time
There's a river to consider after all

No time   no hours   no decades   no millennia.
No   I cannot dump cans of creamed corn
and turkey on noodles and offer forth
sustenance again

A bit pre-occupied, we original 100%
who are also 1%, more or less

Simply distracted by sulfide emissions   tar sands   pipelines   foster
care   polar bears   hydro-fracking   and the playlist deeply intoning
Superman never made any money . . .

River   river   river   Our river
Map of the Milky Way
reflection of stars
whence all life commenced

100% of all life on our planet

River in the middle   Mississippi
not the East Coast Hudson where this all started
waterway Max Fleischer's team lushly rendered
via the wonder of Technicolor

Emerging from an underwater lair
a Mad Scientist we comprehend as indigenous
has lost his signifiers (no braids, no blanket)
but we recognize him
A snappy dresser who flashes a maniac grin
he is not   *not*   your TV Indian

Ignoble Savage ". . . and I still say Manhattan
rightfully belongs to my people"
Superman "Possibly   but just what
do you expect us to do about it?"

Occupy   Occupy   Worked for the 99
Occupy   Re-occupy   Alcatraz and Wounded Knee

Sorry   somehow now I've too much time
Flow   flow   flow both ways   story-history-story
There's a river that considers us after all

All time   all hours   all decades   all millennia

River   river   river
I never   never   never—but that is not to say that I won't ever

NOTES OF PRE-OCCUPIED DIGRESSION: Descendants of the indigenous population of the United States remain just a tad less than 1% of the population according to the 2010 census. If you add Native Hawaiians to the total we are 1.1% of the population. So, we are, more or less, the original 1% as well as the original 100%. As the Occupy movement took hold, indigenous groups continued to struggle to protect our homelands from imminent threats such as the tar sands in Canada and its Keystone pipeline, copper mining in Minnesota and Wisconsin, and hydro-fracking elsewhere— everywhere, it seems. This era of alternative energy has become the new land grab, the new water grab. Indigenous activists are thoroughly pre-occupied with the social and environmental issues I mention and more. Activists can't be everywhere at once—not like Superman. I refer here, of course, to the Crash Test Dummies' 1991 "Superman's Song," which despairs that the world will never see altruism like that of the unpaid hero. In the 1942 cartoon *Electric Earthquake*, an indigenous (but not stereotypically "Indian") Mad Scientist is thwarted, of course, by Superman. At one point Clark Kent admits indigenous land claim as "possibly" valid but says there's nothing the *Daily Planet* can do about it. A shrewd Tesla wannabe, our villain attempts to publish his demands first, then occupies Lois Lane while toppling Manhattan skyscrapers. You can see this beauty all over the Internets.

Curatorial Statement for *Apocalyptic Poetics*

You describe just what you fear. You imagine 99% of the human population just drops dead. You imagine they curl and rot where they drop. Plants die, strange plants spring up, new animals appear, old animals disappear. You imagine this in some future. You imagine a now. You can yet vibrate the hive, cough up rafts of plastic, find time for reprieve, cry out for justice, own the apocalypse before it owns you. You imagine a past. A past as a virgin land, rich loam, bottomland—it was all just waiting there, going to waste, before. Before was just after—after 99% of the living dropped dead, unwept, went back to the earth where they lay. Strange plants sprang up, new animals appeared, old animals disappeared. We walk on the bridge of bones our ancestors left, their bodies fed the great over-bloom of America where we are 1% of the 5% who eat nearly everything. All just as you fear. Yet we are still here.

At the Anachronism Fair

Wonder of a man
balances on his bald head
ice in massive aquamarine blocks   yes
but wisp-thin sculpted figures   too
You, my children,   hear droplets
smell what straw   dust   crowds
sweat and water mixed
make of a hot country day
before you throw your lives
into light boxes
sensory deprivation tanks
for the masses
(me too) who
float here
all eyes and ears
all nostril flare shut off
no huff   no whiff
in the great round now
where our senses grow obsolete
anachronistic   curiosities for other futures
Wonder of it all   child   will be how
you'll know your *need-to-breathe*
(when at last you two meet)
the one you'll pull like breath
your lung-gasping stuff
your not-enough your not-enough

MIX TAPE
AS DIDACTIC

Indigenous Elvis Works the Medicine Line

Indigenous Elvis toes an invisible boundary
signed into being, there but not there

Indigenous Elvis works the border crossing
laser scan checks your tribal ID
lifts your hatch and checks your stash
of saskatoons and Hutterite rugs
gently crooning

Wayah hay ya together . . .
can't go on together hay yah
suspicious minds . . . Wayah hay ya together . . .

stuck as a needle, skipped as a disk.
Wayah hay ya together . . .
Caught in a trap . . . together

Indigenous Elvis works the border crossing
leans deeply into the window
wafts his manly scent a moment
before he asks
This your car?
Where you from?

Indigenous Elvis unhitches your
inhibitions so you giggle
I'm from Minnesota,
it's my husband's car,
I—I'm married.

Indigenous Elvis breathes deeply
through one nostril
squints away   waves *okay*
while you struggle with the gears
his voice rich in your ears

Wayah hay ya together . . .
Doncha, hay ya, doncha . . .
do anything but . . .
Wayah hay yah together . . .

Indigenous Elvis works the border crossing
toes the invisible boundary signed into being
birthed by a signature
there but not there

Big Medicine

Doncha, hay ya, doncha . . .
do anything but . . . go on together
wayah hay yah . . . with suspicious minds . . .

He dances to a flash
to an indigo tune
to blue suede blues—
Wayah hay ya together . . .
dances to a dot you can't help but watch
dwindles to a shimmy
in your rearview mirror
wayah hay yah hay . . .

Rise Up Fallen

Descent does not have to seal
suck air   subordinate   but
We   I inform   *are falling*

You in gray-blue of elevator atmosphere—
quiet   but elevator quiet is not quiet

Rushed   we fall silent
we glance up   remain elevated
on an elevator
that's going down
with its name meaning to lift us up

Your years on you like polish
your smoothness my weakness
your glance—your eyes on   off   up
down   so smoothly

Drawn to you   to kiss   to clasp
Doors open fast
We rise all fallen

we never   I mean I   you   vibration & voice

back against your chest   me   hot-eyed   burst branches

red-flamed for you   or it was just fall

we never said   I mean I   never

don't take it the wrong   I mean I   taped it all wrong

or right   now   wanted it right   I mean I   wanted now

then   that's all that tape   meant

then   that's all   we meant

I mean I   would never say no

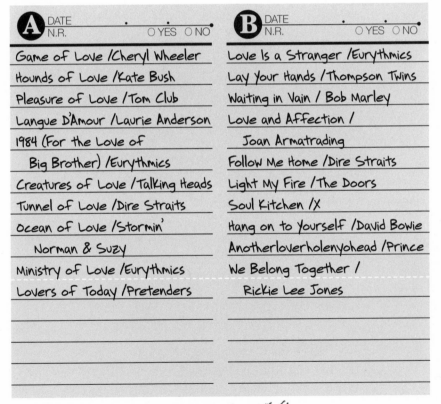

A DATE   N.R.   O YES   O NO

Game of Love /Cheryl Wheeler
Hounds of Love /Kate Bush
Pleasure of Love /Tom Club
Langue D'Amour /Laurie Anderson
1984 (For the Love of
  Big Brother) /Eurythmics
Creatures of Love /Talking Heads
Tunnel of Love /Dire Straits
Ocean of Love /Stormin'
  Norman & Suzy
Ministry of Love /Eurythmics
Lovers of Today /Pretenders

B DATE   N.R.   O YES   O NO

Love Is a Stranger /Eurythmics
Lay Your Hands /Thompson Twins
Waiting in Vain / Bob Marley
Love and Affection /
  Joan Armatrading
Follow Me Home /Dire Straits
Light My Fire /The Doors
Soul Kitchen /X
Hang on to Yourself /David Bowie
Anotherloverholenyohead /Prince
We Belong Together /
  Rickie Lee Jones

Maxell UDS-II 90 Of & Other Tunes   1986

Charger

Oh Wanton   Oh Salome
what was it you wanted?

How sexy
the head
you called for
you got   dead head
you got it off
off that big mouth
crying in the desert   crying
just desserts
on a platter   a silver charger
charged you

Oh sullen   Oh swollen tongue
and rolling eyes turned back
stilled   indifferent   beyond ecstasy
beyond your gaze

Was it what you wanted?
Oh Wanton   Oh Salome

Do You Like Women, Andrea Carlson,
mixed media on paper, 2011

Incantation on a Frank Big Bear Collage

Bar the windows the Red Owl looming into view
cut by bars stripes from the American flag
Bar the eyes but not the breasts
cut from marble pale nudes out of Art History books
Bar the luscious behind of Marilyn Monroe
Cut the cut body-builder the honey-baked ham
the helix sliced into recombinant Christ
Bar the windows the Red Owl looming into view
cut by bars stripes from the American flag
Bar the warriors on the Wallowing Bull work
Cut the Bog Man so he sits right on Custer's face
Bar emblems and icons and emblem-o-graphy
Cut the Blue Period into the blues guitar
Bar the windows the Red Owl looming into view
cut by bars stripes from the American flag
Bar the door to your studio—photographers get in still
Cut happy Anne Frank into newsreel out of *Guernica*
Bar Gertrude Stein and her little dog too!
Cut the death stars from cosmic maps and eclipse them.
Bar the windows the Red Owl looming into view
cut by bars stripes from the American flag
Bar the Sepia-Toned Warrior and the horse he rode in on
Cut the lines curves tones that say *It's full of stars*
Bar the windows the Red Owl looming into view
cut by bars stripes from the American flag
Bar the fringe on the two-hide dress
Cut the sneak-up dancer into action
Bar the wheel spokes and the battle scene
Cut curve of the rubber glove to a dial-up lovely child
Bar the windows the Red Owl looming into view
cut by bars stripes from the American flag

Bar the lines in my poem the lines of my smile
Cut clean with keen comment slashed and clashed colors
Bar the windows the Red Owl looming into view
cut by bars stripes from the American flag

Time Zones (Red Owl), Frank Big Bear,
paper, photo squares, 2013

Little Spirit Will Not Be Caught

I'm a sky wink
a little afraid of the way
you're the pearl of my eye

My teeth chatter
when you breathe so close to me
fog my thoughts without defrost

I used to—
think
with the pink muscle in me
bubbles of thoughts
iridescent wonderings

Now that's all gone to fog
Since you rescued me reused me saved me
and leashed me to the wall

When they get too close
I let them know
I'm a circus dog
trapped in a shell clasp

They figure out fast
in a snap
—Like that!

Little Spirit, Jim Denomie, abalone
and found-object mask, 2012

Exhibit A

Flickering sound and that's what's
beneath my lids
Loop that depth of black
firecracker crack of colors
pressed lava hot floaty
moats in a girl's eyes opening
to yarn on sticks circa 1970s
now only shreds offered to trees, bird-stripped,
de-striped, fallen into hallows,
barked over into gray-green clean of any, all, every

God's Eye, Heid E. Erdrich, acrylic
yarn, popsicle sticks, film shot beneath
closed lids, birds, time, 2015

Exhibit B—Bear

because your   every-damn-thing-seeing mind
drank the clouds off november   and crawled off to die
and winter erased even your name
we stared north   gray words for cold   our mouths formed
nothing more   nothing to recover
    how you did it no one   no
old story   one we forget at times   you took a form
insistence   what pushes ice aside   tubers green-drive
green and return   rank as ramps   rank as bear risen
red bear   wheels for eyes   everyday witness   sun spun
love sickness   grin gleam   every-blest-thing-seeing eye
how it is to be alive   to be   alive to be alive

Misko-makwa, Jonathan Thunder,
spray paint, salvaged plastic wheels,
and other garden items, on 20-foot
wood-framed garage wall, 2015

Exhibit F

Aurora borealis in a box constructed of North Dakota maps
held in attendant hands in saffron drape
no face no figure shown
as trafficked women speak:
   . . . the flare-struck sky in the evening appears
            like an orange version of the Northern Lights.
and a chorus of the missing tell us:
During overcast days, the clouds reflect a pervasive carroty flickering
while viewers engage live communal painting
triggering flickering orange light that reveals
a map. We tap the map but it will not show us where.

Carroty Flickering, Heid E. Erdrich, aurora
borealis, quotes from Talli Nauman, *Native Sun
News*, trafficked women, the missing, orange
light, the rest of us, 2015

Curatorial Note for Exhibit C

Exhibit C: Mitochondrial haplogroup C and Y-chromosome haplogroup C walk into a bar, 2016, deploys mixed-media installation including audio of Ojibwe language narrative and text in English to produce an immersive environment where viewers soon discover they will not easily digest the work. The installation resists providing context except in a few instances: casual references to haplogroups A, B, D, and X, and a banner printed with a quote from Jessica Kolopenuk that states, *There are lessons embedded in* wiindigo *stories like this one. Unlike what dna.ancestry.com asserts—that our history is written in our DNA—lessons are not.* The locale created here, a social space for those of Native American ancestry, leaves questions with few answers in its glasses, matches, and drink coasters printed with a logo for *Bar Q.*

Exhibit Q—Q-Code Found Poem

Found while reading the Wikipedia entry for "Q Code"

QRA: What coast is that?

QRB: What is your distance?   A: QRB5   *Very distant*

QRN: Are the atmospherics strong?

QRM: Are you being interfered with?

QRA: What coast is that?   A: QRA5   *A distant coast*

QRD: Where are you bound for?

QRF: Where are you bound from?

QRG: What line do you belong to?   A: -- .- -.- .-- .-   *Makwa*

QRC: What is your true bearing?   A: .. -. -.. --- --- -.. .- --   *indoodam*

QRK1: Unreadable   A: -.... .- .-. -.-. .-.. .- -.   *bear clan*

QRJ: How many words have you to send?

QRK: How do you receive me?   A: QRK1   *unreadable*

QSW/QSX: Shall I increase/decrease my spark frequency?

QRN: Are the atmospherics strong?

QRL: Are you busy?

QRJ: How many words have you to send?

QRM: Are you being interfered with?   A: QRM   *manmade interference*

QRJ: How many words have you to send?

QRK: How do you receive me?   A: QRK5   *perfectly*

QSW/QSX: Shall I increase/decrease my spark frequency?

QRJ: How many words have you to send?   A: .- .-.. .-.. / .-- --- .-. -.. ...

All of the words

QRN: Are the atmospherics strong?   A: QRN   *the atmospherics are strong*

"We're supposed to be hyperaware of
'atmospherics,'" Morris told me, pinpointing the
sticky problem of apophenia, its grace and peril.
—Katy Waldman, Slate, September 16, 2014

mix-ward stages   Joan Armatrading accepts and bargains both

next on deck   Annie Lennox's anger turns to regret

Grace Jones tells me

that sh*t's wet   warm leatherette waft   ghost sweat scent

never meant to hurt   then

drop in open window   your dodge

deny it now

Ⓐ DATE ・ ・ N.R. ○ YES ○ NO	Ⓑ DATE ・ ・ N.R. ○ YES ○ NO
Never Lied To My Lover	If I Did I Would Admit It
Time Will Tell / Bob Marley	Love Alive / Heart
If I . . . / Squeeze	Haunted / The Pogues
I Could Give You / Eurythmics	Never Took No / John Cale
The Walk / Eurythmics	Broken English / Marianne Faithfull
Kind Words / Joan Armatrading	Pleasure and Pain / Divinyls
In the Eye / Suzanne Vega	Private Life / Grace Jones
Guilt / Marianne Faithfull	Brain Drain / Marianne Faithfull
Dancing Barefoot / Patti Smith	Faded Flowers / Shriekback
Mercy Street / Peter Gabriel	Gravity's Angel / Laurie Anderson
Carolina in My Mind / Melanie	Running to Stand Still / U2
Peace in Mind / Joan Armatrading	

Maxell II 90 Never Lied . . . But if I did   circa 1988

The Four Findings of Agent H

The Mother

As a subject   she yielded little
though her brow told
she was a mother—she knew
the necessity of giving others pain
When questioned   her rigid attitude
suggested everything suspected
She implied a mind compartmental
component contraption—her mode
Tiny claws in me clutched truth
though she would go on mirroring back
my every inquest
She never did speak,   of course   She never
even showed her mouth   Still her voice filtered
mote-like   particulate as dust
Everything she meant
she meant though arch and ceaseless glint
So no   she did not speak and yet I sensed
as if a flare of instinct toward water
her flowing great volume
her acute determination
her molten will to express

The Mother, Louise Erdrich,
found-object construction, 2015

47

The Woman

Deliberate inquiry answered.
She just repeats herself.
Of course   she says   *Of course.*
You can ask her anything,
she issues forth the same
oblique agreement   *Of course.*
Or does she mean we asked
the exact question she'd expect?
If I tried to redirect   she'd pause,
but pretty soon she'd turn me.
Of course   So rather than inquire,
I am observing   Her dress,
comportment   culpability   her ribbons,
or filaments   distract
—the eye dilates   defaults to static.
Trickle or swell? Difficult to tell
the meaning of her flux   her expansive
reach and then distinct contraction.
I admit she has me flummoxed.
Yet   I must report   *Of course.*

Story of a Woman, Louise Erdrich, acrylic
on canvas, typescript on paper, 2015

Four Women

Certainly they tell us all we need
in flow and direction   She reddens,
goes golden   grows blue and blackens
in power born of sorrow or strength
or both   why not? No one is limited
to one   How many women   truly
live as fewer than four?

Four Women, Aza Erdrich, acrylic
on canvas, 2015

Agent Blue

Trick of the eye or sleight of hand
her *modus operandi*
her competence and confidence
commend her as capable   but culpable?
What if she fixed the workings
of this mystery   took it all apart and held
all calls long enough to commit it all?
Never an angel but an agent of doom—
Or no   no   of course not
Let's look further   let's continue
until we fix the author of these actions
until we exhaust our agency

Agent Blue, Pallas Erdrich,
electronic media series, 2015

Agency Apophany* www.agencyapophany
serves as a virtual gallery for images related
to Heid E. Erdrich's poems. Here you can
hear the poet read from, "The Findings of
Agent H"—part of a 2014 installation project
around Louise Erdrich's artwork presented
by Bockley Gallery in Minneapolis. You can
also hear Louise Erdrich's phone messages
for Agent H, who is on the case, interviewing
suspects, determined to solve this and other
Mysteries of Life.

*Apophany is a mistaken epiphany.

Mix Tape Didactic . . . *Break Up 2*

I mean I   broke up with you

A DATE N.R. ● ● ● ○ YES ○ NO	**B** DATE N.R. ● ● ● ○ YES ○ NO
For My Lover / Tracy Chapman	Telling Me Lies / Emmylou Harris
Tunnel of Love / Dire Straits	Why'd Ya Do It / Marianne Faithful
Try a Little Tenderness /	Smoking Gun / Robert Cray
Otis Redding	Tell It Like It Is / Aaron Neville
Cry to Me / Solomon Burke	Dazed and Confused / Led Zeppelin
I Wanna Be Your Dog /	Summer Oy / Cheryl Wheeler
The Stooges	It Makes No Difference / The Band
Love Is Strange /	Don't Break My Heart / UB40
Mickey & Sylvia	Rip It Up / Orange Juice
Give Me Back My Man / B-52's	
Don't Talk / 10,000 Maniacs	
Ship of Fools / Robert Plant	
With or Without You / U2	
Why Don't You Quit Leaving	
Me Alone / Rosanne Cash	

Maxell XLII-S 90 Mouse Mix 1988

Autobiography as Mix Tape for Lady Mon de Green

All that I read I misread   All that I heard I misheard

My skull holds a bowl of spark soup imprinted with grooves that ripple briefly
and remove their paths so faint traces remain   yes   As if sparks in dark
liquids could know/guess our first and most ancient medium—mud and sticks
or no   our hands   the thumb of the beloved   gesture trace—mother's
touch   Creator's breath

What I have to say I've said
       in glyph and graph   incised   inscribed   sprayed   scratched
       pen and pencil   ink and etching and charcoal with my hand as
       template for mammoth back and pregnant mare—

All that I read I misread   All that I heard I misheard

Don't go out tonight, it's bound to take your life, there's a bathroom on the right
. . . Oh, Benny, she's really wonderful, oh, Benny, she's really mean . . . Don't shake it
baby, lay the real thing on me. The Church of Mellow is such a holy place to be . . .

In the old folks home they'll know which grooves my needle sticks   They'll
hear my full Archive of Mixed Grooves—a mystery to the youth who marvels
closely at cassettes and deck then says
    . . . music made with ribbons and magnets—what alchemy is this?

What I have to say I've said
       with correction fluid   x-acto knife   wax and bray   with
       stylus and scribe   Commodore Fat Mac   origami   rubber
       stamp   iron-on   calligraphy   Etch A Sketch   and nib and quill and
       crayon—

She's got erector boots, it's not her suit, you know I read it in a magazine, oh, oh,
. . . Blinded by the light, revved up like a douche, you know the rumor in the night
. . . Dirty Dean and the Thunder Chiefs . . .

The Archive of Mixed Grooves and all these labels meant to prove the thesis of
my love   Remember   I gave one to you?   But I kept one   too   I had the kind
of faith that duplicates even in those days when we gave it all away

What I have to say I've said
        via telex   Teletype   facsimile/fax   radio   in vinyl
        postcard   sticky note   through the curled 12-foot cord
        of old-school teen-line land-line telephone

And then? We just let it go   no record left of what it was so needed to be said

There was no Curator of Ephemera   though if there were
she would be me

        my coil of copper   a heavy sheen in my hand—recording wire scored
        at an estate sale for "Six Generations of Hoarders!" stacked high-fi
        on top of hi-fi atop wireless routers and "Project-O-Scope" beneath
        the dusty buttress of slide viewers number one and two and many
        more   "Pana-Vue" and Sharper Image wireless TV   analog tuned
        to perpetual static now   It comforts me somehow—the white noise
        of before times   We waited eternities for the grainy waver of TVs
        Something called "warming up" we found the patience for—

Well you promised to love me completely baby—whatever happened to you?

What I have to say I've said   I've fed the Ephemeral Fountain at the center of
the New Museum's Most Recent Wing where all our instant messages reprint
themselves in endless flickering splashing   twinkling   chatting   blathering and
ranting   scattering like schools of tetras at the plop of trolls and stalkers

The limitlessness of light—light once the essence of ephemeral—now how we
groove the spark soup
All that I read I misread   All that I heard I misheard

What I have to say I've   *light all the love that I*
What I have to say I've   *light all the love that I*

What I have to say I've said with light

What I have to say I've said   yet never made my meaning known

never the same message I sent
something always lost in transmit
lost and transformed
by the limits of the limitless
that blinks back your I plus verb plus you

light OF the love

That   I found

THE NEW ARCHAIC

The Buzz

Do you remember, My Love,
the buzz, as you drew me to you
in the over-green of our first garden?
Do you remember the humming?
You matched your hot palm
to my smooth cool palm
amidst a mad tumbling:
cosmos and sage and asters
alive with bees, dripping
and dropping on my dress,
your red beard against my breast,
sweetly rumbling, *Oh, Honey Suckle.*
We pulsed and beat that hot staccato,
we swayed to drones' doom, a swoon
on swelling air, the now-rare music of bees.
And we were ever so young.
And so we never were stung.

Lexiconography 1/Clothes Pins

for Zhaabadiis Naano-zhoomaanke miinawaa Otchingwanigan

We used them long ago, clothespins.
We can taste them still, clenched in our teeth.

We pinched wooden clothespins on clouds,
lines of a little child's clothes,
lines of a man's clothes, heavy denim,
and a woman's clothes—
fine white fabric of nightgowns,
under-things, blouses in clouds,
and sun seen through clouds.

We plucked the clothespins,
collapsed the clouds of clothing.
Wind combed the water, came crying.
We collected the clothes, the clouds.

We used them long ago, clothespins.
We taste them still, clenched in our teeth.

"Lexiconography 1" is available
at Broadsided Press as a
downloadable work of art
designed by Meghan Kane.
"Lexiconography 1" is translated
by Margaret Noodin as part of
a series of poem-as-language-
lesson collaborations Erdrich and
Noodin engaged.

Aabjito'ikidowinan 1/Anishinaabe Language Lesson 1

translations by Margaret Noodin

We used them long ago, clothespins.
Mewenzha n'gii ziinaakwa'igemi
Long ago we clothes-pinned

We can taste them still, clenched in our teeth.
N'gii gojipidaminan, n'gii ziinibidominan bito-wiibidoning
We tasted them, we squeezed them between our teeth

We pinched wooden clothespins on clouds,
N'gii ziinibidominan aanakwadoon
We pinch clouds

lines of a little child's clothes,
aanziianan miinawaa waabooanan
of diapers and blankets

lines of a man's clothes, heavy denim,
miikanot miinawaa bitomiikanotan
of pants and underpants

and a woman's clothes—
gaawiin ziibaaskasiigoodenan
dresses without jingles

fine white fabric of nightgowns,
nookaa niibing nibaawiiyan
soft summer sleepwear

under-things, blouses in clouds,
bidaankwaad biiskaanaan
dawn clouds to wear

and sun seen through clouds.
miinawaa waasenaakwe'aanakwad giiskanaan
bright clouds of noon to take off.

We plucked the clothespins,
Ziinaakwa'iganan n'gii asiginaminan
We gathered clothespins

collapsed the clouds of clothing.
N'gii bisikiigaminan biizikiigan-aanakwadoon
We folded clouds of clothing

Wind combed the water, came crying.
Madweyaasin giwayaan obaasbinaakwaanan
The sound of the wind combed them dry.

We collected the clothes, the clouds.
Aanakwadoon miinawaa biizikiigan n'gii asiginaminan
We gathered the clouds and clothes

We used them long ago, clothespins.
Mewenzha n'gii ziinaakwa'igemi
Long ago we clothes-pinned

We taste them still, clenched in our teeth.
N'gii gojipidaminan, n'gii ziinibidominan bito-wiibidoning
We tasted them, we squeezed them between our teeth

Laundress

Given over to love,
she un-balls the socks,

lets fall debris of days,
leaf litter, sand grain,

slub of some sticky substance,
picks it all for the sake

of the stainless tub
of the gleaming new front loader.

Given over to love long ago, when her own
exasperated moan bounced off

the quaint speckled enamel
of the old top loader

vowing: she'd do this always and well.
She fell in love then, she fell in line—

in a march of millions, you pair them,
two by two, you marry the socks.

Shepherd

Given over to love,
he scrapes the plates,

lets fall debris of meals,
crumb shatter, wrack of grains,

slag of some greasy sustenance,
picks it all for the sake

of the stainless tall tub
of the gleaming new dishwasher.

Given over to love long ago, when his own
exasperated oath bounced off

the quaint speckled enamel
of the old double sink—

the gate to his herder's instinct so
keen on constant strays, on lookout

for the lost ewes of cups, the lambs
of ramekins, the damn ram of frying pan.

He swore. His vow: do this always and well.
He fell in love then, he held the line—

against a wash of millions. He'd do them.
Day by day, he would husband the flock.

Dying Well

Refused the sugar-soaked sponge,
the offer to read aloud a childhood book,
the trembling water glass catching the light.
Refused with a stutter of expression
the hesitant knock at the door,
the one more goodbye.
Waved away embrace
and tender whispers days before,
the day the black-vested Holy Man
touched a last fragrant offering
of cedar to his brow. He asked for nothing.
All comforts he gave back.
He smiled to listen to them laugh.
He let the loved ones know, at last,
with one word: No.
He would not distract his dying, fill his time.
Already the fullness of life squeezed
into his room—he'd send it ahead place by place,
notion by notion, and face by face.
He said no. He had work to do.
His son understood, cleared the room. He withdrew.

Lexiconography 2—It Was Cloudy

for the Nichols and Nyholm dictionary, pages 158–159

Cloud beings come laughing, comical,   ~~aanakwad vii;~~ biidaapi vai;
They come singing, through the clouds: *biidwewidam* vai
morning white clouds, a good color.   *waabishkaanakwad* vii;
minwaandemagad vii
Springtime is a comedy.   *gagiibaadaatesemagad* vii
Cloud beings come telling news, clouds   *biidaajimo* vai
come as wind from a certain place.   *ondaanimad* vii
Cloud beings come to sit comfortably,   *minwabi* vai
companion, in Summer.   *wiijiiwaagan* na
Red clouds come, colored a certain way: *miskwaanakwad* vii
copper coins, hot coals, they come with a light.   *zhooniyaans* na; ~~akakanzhe ni;~~
biidaazakwanenjige vai
Fall dark clouds come into view.   *makadeyaanakwad* vii
They come in anger, storm clouds,   ~~biijigidaazo vai;~~ *zegaanakwad* vii
a ball-headed club, a war club, coals again, coffee.   *bikwaakwado-bagamaagan* ni;
akakanzhe ni;

Winter comes, contests continually.   *Biboon bakinaage apane*

Aabjito'ikidowinan 2/Anishinaabe Language Lesson 2

translations by Margaret Noodin

Cloud beings come laughing, comical,
Aanakwadoog bidaapiwag, wawiyadenimwaad,

They come singing, through the clouds:
Biidnagamowaad, zhiibaanakwad

morning white clouds, a good color.
Minowaabishkaanakwad bidaabanong.

Springtime is a comedy.
Ziigwan gagiibaadaatesemagad.

Cloud beings come telling news, clouds
Aanakwadoog biidaajimowag,

come as wind from a certain place.
ondaanimaanakwad.

Cloud beings come to sit comfortably,
Aanakwadoog biindigewag, minwabiwaad,

companion, in Summer.
wiijii'iwewaad, niibinong.

Red clouds come, colored a certain way:
Biidaanakwadoog, miskwaazhe:

copper coins, hot coals, they come with a light.
miskwaabikizhooniyaansag, gizhokakanzhean, biidaazakwanenjigewaad.

Fall dark clouds come into view.
Makadeyaanakwad binaagwad daagwaaging.

They come in anger, storm clouds,
Biijigidaazowag, zegaanakwadoog

a ball-headed club, a war club, coals again, coffee.
bikwaakwado-bagamaagan, bagamaagan, kakanzhean
                         miinawaa, makademashkikiwaaboo
Winter comes, contests continually.
Biboon bakinaage apane.

What Gathers

Twisting stems weave
green to red against leaves
raindrop-shaped and tender,
shelter for blue-black berries.

We taste pure purple. We gather.
We touch our tongues to juice
we've asked to grow for us.

We children in our northern gardens
gather dark sweetness of saskatoons,
indigenous fruit that taught Ojibwe
beadwork patterns of vine and leaf
—winter's longing, worked by hand,
reminder of a hot day to come,
promise bright against threat.

Doubtless that was part of it:
what was gathering long ago,
the rush of other, the great change,
foods, woods, bison, prairie,
gods, songs, goods,
all about to alter.

We touch our tongues to summer.
What gathers now we do not know—
some low rumble on the globe's edge.

We gather. Nail tips and lips
stained, we do as our blood asks.

These berries the same berries
our ancestors plucked,
rolling a thumb against the curved edge,
teasing ripeness, readiness,
old ladies joking: Find me a man
can handle a woman like that!

Swoon in July sun, in sensual acts,
the fruit asks. We do as it wishes, we gather,
chilled still by long winter—
always just behind us, always just ahead.

Stars, Seeds, Signs, Ours

Ashkibagiziibiing/St. Peter/St. Paul—1837

We return here ever

Deep and still with icy stars—
Sky above our new home the same sky
as over our old lands north of the river

We move and they move   Long Knives behind
Dakota before   We leave the good seed
manoomin   the food that grows on water

Here above the big river our leaders dream
a place we can be safe   but visions come of a time
to come   our children making signs on white pine

Flat Mouth will mark and Elder Brother
Young Bison will mark and others' names
will grow strange in new language

We move and they move   Long Knives behind
Dakota before   We leave the good seed
manoomin   the food that grows on water

Deep and still with icy stars—
Sky above our new home the same sky
as over our old lands north of the river

From this spot   we vision our gardens
mandamin and okosomin and their sisters
We left the white pines north for this river

Bear Heart will mark and Hole in the Day
Strong Ground will mark and others' names
will grow strange in new language

We move and they move   Long Knives behind
Dakota before   We leave the good seed
manoomin   the food that grows on water

Here above the big river   our leaders dream
a place we can be safe   but visions come of a time
to come our children sign White Pine Treaty

Deep and still with icy stars—
Sky above our new home the same sky
as over our old lands north of the river

We stop here and look back—
White banks and slough and clouds
stacked in layers of forever

Our rice beds left   but not our seeds
Not our stars and not our right
to hunt and fish and gather

We return here ever.

A Loud Green Dreaming

While I am dreaming
laundry flops noisily in the dryer,
tumbles into a vividness:
drum and thunder, fragrant wetness.

We run a green path,
swim a river brown as root beer,
sleep curled together where stars stoop,
kiss our lids, lift us slightly—

We startle.

We tumble.
                    I catch you, my girl.

When I wake there's a note in two inks,
one green, embellished for emphasis:

Wake up, Sleepyhead!
Don't Fall Back.

Drum and thunder cease with a beep.

I gather armfuls of cloth,
still aware of your warmth,
holding you near, dream music in my ear,
tumble of your pockets full of green lint
and polished rocks.   I promise:

We come back to earth,
every time, but the last time.
Go ahead, I can catch you,
every time until the last time.

In between, dear, our dreams mean to make us

                            learn to love the fall.

Ombigwewe Ozhaawaashkwaa Bwaajige/ Anishinaabemowin Lesson 3

translations by Margaret Noodin

While I am dreaming
Epiichi bwaajigeyaanh
While I dream

laundry flops noisily in the dryer,
epiichii gwewinan ombigwewebide bengwaamigad
while the laundry makes noise drying

tumbles into a vividness:
niisakseaazhe
tumbling apart brightly

drum and thunder, fragrant wetness.
dewegaade, jiingwe, minomaagoz
drumming, thundering, fragrant

We run a green path,
Bimibatooyaang ozhaawaashkwaa miikanens
We run a green path

swim a river brown as root beer,
bigizoyaang minagwaakimizhabo ziibing
we swim a sarsaparilla river

sleep curled together where stars stoop,
giiwitaawiipende enji anongonsag endaawaad
curled in sleep together in the home of stars

kiss our lids, lift us slightly—
jiindaanan shkiinzhigwewinan, ombabiganaagoziyaang
our eyelids kissed, we are lifted

We startle.
Maamkadendamoyaang.

We tumble.
Niisakseyaang.

            I catch you, my girl.
            G'debibzhin, ndo'kwesens.

When I wake there's a note in two inks,
Pii gaashkoziyaanh, niizh enaandegmazinaigens teg
When I wake, a two-colored note is there

one green, embellished for emphasis:
ozhawaashkwaande, maashkobiigaade
one green, embellished

Wake up Sleepyhead!
Gaashkozin Ayekozidip!
Wake up Sleepyhead!

Don't Fall Back.
Gego nibaake miinwaa.
Don't sleep again.

Drum and thunder cease with a beep.
Boondewegaade, boonjiingwe . . . biip
Drumming ceases, thundering ceases . . . beep.

I gather armfuls of cloth,
Nd'asiganan gidigiiganan
I gather cloth

still aware of your warmth,
geyabi gikendan gizhiyin,
still knowing your warmth

holding you near, dream music in my ear,
gaashidinin, noondaamaan bwaamomadwechige taawageng
holding you near, hearing dream music in my ears

tumble of your pockets full of green lint
gdo'biindaaganan mooshkine ozhaawaashkwaa wiiyaksen
your pockets full of green lint

and polished rocks.   I promise:
miinawaa zhoonyaabikoon.   Nd'waawiindamaage:
and rocks that shine.   I promise:

We come back to earth,
Aki biskaabiyaang,
To earth we return,

every time, but the last time.
endaaso ezhewebag, gaawiin shkwaatch.
each time, but the last.

Go ahead, I can catch you,
Gikendaan, gd'gaashkidebibzhin
Know it, I can catch you

every time until the last time.

endaaso ezhewebag, biiniish shkwaatch.
each time, until the last.

In between, dear, our dreams mean to make us
Bitooying, bazgem, pii bwaajigeying
In between, dear, when we dream

        learn to love the fall.
        minwendaamaang ezhi-baangishying.
        we know the love of falling.

Manidoo Giizhikens / Little Spirit Cedar Tree

Who makes a shawl of her own arms

Who wraps herself up
holding the last warmth
of someone she loved once
one hundred or two hundred or seven hundred years since

We lift our faces to her many faces

Whose hair frights and stands into the wind
terrified or terrifying
we only know when close
how to take her pose
which changes as women change
day by day by day

We lift our faces to her many faces
We hold our bodies to her many bodies

Whose way with wind makes a call
we must answer must slip on tilting rocks
pass between a boulder portal
to her side her knees her waist

We lift our faces to her many faces
We hold our bodies to her many bodies
We give our voices to her many voices

We fall to her in our need
to breathe her astringency
her cleansing medicine

We lift our faces to her many faces
We hold our bodies to her many bodies
We give our voices to her many voices
We gift sweetgrass   asema   stones   tokens

We take away no sureness of her
aware only that time whirls waves
makes bone-bleached sculptures of us all

We do not believe that she is small
she who brinks the greatness of creation
the greatness of the lake while tied to rock
grown small in spirit maybe but no
she holds stone to stone she composes the cliff
We know her then we do not know her

We hold our bodies to her many bodies
We give our voices to her many voices

Whose tortured form twists
away at once and ever back
her pain an emblem of release
she gives over to the waves
waves that change as she changes
one day gray the next vivid as prism

We give our voices to her many voices
We gift sweetgrass   asema   stones   tokens

Whose torso blown with holes
suffers no loss but fills
her crevices sensual as pleasure
etched with florescence of lichen
She hides and shows at once
She chooses all and gives all away

We hold our bodies to her many bodies
We lift our faces to her many faces

And this is why the painter
addresses her for fifty years
sees her new in every light
Every hour on every day a year can make

We lift our faces to her many faces
she returns a thousand forms
and we have been every one of them

We lift our faces to her many faces and she remains

Spirit Tree: Survivor, Hazel Belvo,
acrylic on canvas, 2013

Curatorial Statement on *The Long Gallery*

Installation in *The Long Gallery* works in reverse. Here you see the backs of things: the stitches flecked as pelts; bleed-through of obscured figures; cat fluff–filled canvasses; brushed notes, titles, dates, dedications; bunch of sage; happy face of two-screw hang kit; dulls eyes of bolts; cross of clear sweet pine; thumb prints and palm prints; all between the struggle of ragged selvages held against their will by staple gangs.

What draws me to this body, drew me to this body: the sense and scents, richness of linseed, oat of gesso, dust of charcoal, pigment fragrant and diverse, viridian smell of melon, carnelian chip of nail enamel, any tube of blue on my lips a numb kiss. You get my drift.

Impossibly narrow, *The Long Gallery* admits only one. Works appear for an indefinite yet finite time. The Curator is finite. Perfectly lit, *The Long Gallery* is mine.

Author's Notes

A word about QR codes: Many of the poems in this collection come out of my experience of working with visual artists as a curator, of making collaborative poemeos (a term my sister Louise and niece Pallas coined for videos from poems), and of my own interest in the visual appearance of work on the page. In 2011 I applied for funding from the Minnesota State Arts Board to make book trailers with award-winning filmmaker Elizabeth Day and lauded animator Jonathan Thunder. Since then, we have worked together on eight short films, including two animated Ojibwe-language works. You can see some of these films and learn more about the folks who helped me make them by reading the QR codes in this book with your mobile device.

One of the most ephemeral of media phenomena, QR codes became accessible to the general public in 2011. By 2012 bloggers declared the QR code dead. They have been declared dead annually since then. Long live the QR code!

A word about visual art images: below several of the poems, you will see the titles of artworks, most of which are available to view via a virtual gallery on my website, www.heiderdrich.com, or at www.agencyapophany.com. Two of these images, however, *God's Eye* and *Carroty Flickering*, are held not in a gallery but in my own mind's eye.

A word about translations: the poems in this book that are accompanied by Ojibwe (Anishinaabe) language translations are tutorials in the form of poems from the gracious poet and language teacher Margaret Noodin. Where you see the poem in my English version, then Ojibwe by Noodin, then English by Noodin, you are seeing her teach me the literal translation in our indigenous language (which helps me understand the grammar) followed by a poetic return to English, which helps us both investigate the differences between the languages.

A note of gratitude: this book is composed out of the collaborative spirit that has energized my creative work for the past decade. Within this book are connections to more people than I can thank, but I will try. My gratitude to art makers Carolyn Lee Anderson, Frank Big Bear, Hazel Belvo, Andrea Carlson, Jim Denomie, Angie Erdrich, Aza Erdrich, Louise Erdrich, Pallas Erdrich, Eric Gansworth, and Dyani Whitehawk; dozens of lyric writers and singers; the mixtape queen, Anne Barber; Anishinaabemowin guide Margaret Noodin; filmmaking mentors Trevino Brings Plenty, Elizabeth Day, and Jonathan Thunder; manuscript copy editor Susan Campbell; bookmakers Jeff Rathermel, Todd Thyberg and staff and volunteers at Minnesota Center for Book Arts; Gordon Henry Jr, and the patient staff at Michigan State University Press, especially Kristine Blakeslee for her enthusiastic reception of this quirky collection and her creative direction to designer Erin Kirk New who worked so hard to make this book look like the one inside my head.

And a special thanks to those who regularly lend me their solidarity and strength: John Burke, Todd Bockley, Kate Kysar, and Rosy Simas.

I am grateful for the support of the Minnesota State Arts Board (full credits in poem films) and First People's Fund, which allowed me to work in community. Thank you to colleagues at the institutions who host me as visiting writer and speaker and who make it possible for me to live as a poet.

Thank you all.

A Note about the Art

Mewenzha, long time ago, Andrea Carlson's artwork reminded me of Ojibwe stories of a fierce cannibal creature made of ice. This creature had a name I won't say out loud more than twice. It ate everything. Everyone. To be ravenous and Ojibwe are simultaneous states both historically accurate and antithetical to our way of life. We, both Andrea Carlson and myself, come from a people who lived in ice more months of the year than not. We knew hunger and prepared for it. We fasted. We feasted. We told terrifying stories of how hunger could make monsters of us.

It may not be cultural at all. It may be coincidence that Andrea Carlson's artwork is voracious in a way that I can relate to, or it may be some aesthetic we share from who knows where. But make no mistake, no matter where it comes from, I love her ravenous eye for the detail of the world, the monsters, machines, myths, and human obsessions that make her huge paintings work like stories—unhinged narratives like short films. Her short films work similarly to build motion out of design. I identify with her big eye for the landscape and seascape of her homeland, the Great Lakes coast in northern Minnesota where we Ojibwe became a people and where I go to enlarge my own eye, to expand my own vision, and to understand the vision of other Ojibwe and Minnesota artists. It may be. I do not know. What I do know is that Andrea Carlson is a storyteller.

Mewenzha, long time ago, Andrea Carlson told me that the Ojibwe might have called the first lighthouse they saw "The Wiindigo's Eye"—and I believe her because I can picture how that giant eye of light whose gaze travelled over Chippewa City and upon all who sailed or paddled the shores nearby would seem a hungry searcher, familiar to the Ojibwe people who lived near. I could believe this because we are all hungry searchers.

Andrea Carlson told me that little tale after I had seen, and instantly recognized, a Fresnel lens in her large scale, multi-panel, virtuosic painting *Ink Babel*. I wanted to answer Andrea's work with my own. It is a small offering, but critical context. The images you see throughout this book are from Andrea's *Ink Babel*.

Over the years, I have written several poems inspired by Andrea's work and in response to our conversations about shared obsessions. To honor our connection, and to reference the story she told me, I made a farcically intoned prose poem titled "Curatorial Statement for *Wiindigo Eye*."

In the poem, I read Andrea Carlson's work through the mechanics of the Fresnel lens, which creates light/image through a flat surface and a curved surface in a process of *imaging and non-imaging*. Andrea Carlson's work both images indigenous experience and deliberately creates non-images that viewers might perceive as indigenous or Ojibwe, but that are not derived from Ojibwe culture at all. I do the same in my poem by including texts that are lyrics from the American singing group They Might Be Giants and from a cultural critic, Jessica Kolopenuk, who reveals the cannibalistic impulses in the sale and purchase of services that erroneously identify people as "Native American" based on results of DNA samples. I am playing with the notion that DNA can tell you who you are and that cultural references can be excavated in our artwork to create meaning based on identity.

Mewenzha, long time ago, Andrea Carlson's artwork reminded me of Ojibwe stories of a fierce cannibal creature made of ice. There is only one way to kill the cannibal creature, and it involved hot substances poured down its gullet. I have heard different versions of this story. Sometimes this ice giant is defeated by the trickster, a young gambler, or a little girl. I like to think the girl was the first person to figure out how to slay the monster. I like to think she gambled and tricked him. I like to see similar gambles and tricks at work in Andrea Carlson's paintings and films that say that no matter how hungry you are, you will not eat us. We will eat everything we see and offer it back to you, in exquisitely rendered detail, but you will not eat us in the end. We will trick you if we have to, Andrea Carlson says, but we will survive.

There are two main types of Fresnel lens: imaging and non-imaging. Imaging Fresnel lenses use segments with curved cross-sections and produce sharp images, while non-imaging lenses have segments with flat cross-sections, and do not produce sharp images.

Acknowledgments

The following poems were previously included in publications as noted:

Amythest and Agates	"Manidoo Giizhikens/Little Spirit Cedar Tree"
Broadsided	"Lexiconography 1/Aabjito'ikidowinan 1" (with translations)
Conduit	"Autobiography as Gesture" and "Autobiography as Mix Tape for Lady Mon de Green"
Cream City Review	"Incantation on a Frank Big Bear Collage"
Montreal Prize Global Anthology	"What Gathers"
99 Poems for the 99%	"Pre-Occupied"
North American Review	"Red Star"
Revolver	"These Are My Pearls, This Is My Swine"
The Good Men Project	"Dying Well," "Laundress," and "Shepherd"
The Whale	"Charger" and "Little Spirit Will Not Be Caught"
Thinking Continental	"The Dark Sky Reserve"
Tinder Box Journal	"The Gig of Light" and "The Honey Suckers"
Water-Stone Review	"Boom"
Yellow Medicine Review	"Agent Blue," "Four Women," "Lexiconography 2/Aabjito'ikidowinan 2," "A Loud Green Dreaming/Ombigwewe Ozhaawaashkwaa Bwaajige" (with translations) "The Mother," and "The Woman"

Brief quotes from articles by Brian Gehring, Talli Nauman, Jan Swenson, and Katy Waldman are fully cited within the text. Quotes from Jessica Kolopenuk are from "Wiindigo Incarnate: Consuming 'Native American DNA'," GeneWatch, 2014.

REPRINTS

"Boom" in *North Dakota Is Everywhere*, Center for Regional Studies (2015) "Curatorial Note for Exhibit C," "Curatorial Statement for *Apocalyptic Poetics*," "Curatorial Statement on *The Long Gallery*," "Curatorial Statement for *Wiindigo Eye*," "Exhibit A," "Exhibit B—Bear," "Exhibit F," "Exhibit Q—Q-Code Found Poem," "Findings of Agent H: The Mother," "Findings of Agent H: Four Women," "The Honey Suckers," and "Little Spirit Will Not Be Caught" in *every-blest-thing-seeing-eye*, letterpress and deluxe letterpress editions, Minnesota Center for Book Arts, Minneapolis (2016).

VIDEOS

"Undead Faerie Goes Great with India Pale Ale," DVD issue from *Iron Horse Review* (2015)

RESOURCES

"Exhibit Q—Q-Code Found Poem" was inspired by https://en.wikipedia.org/wiki /Q_code.